COME JOURNEY
WITH ME

COME JOURNEY WITH ME

KEVIE L. ANDERSON

iUniverse, Inc.
Bloomington

COME JOURNEY WITH ME

iUniverse books may be ordered through booksellers or by contacting:

iUniverse
1663 Liberty Drive
Bloomington, IN 47403
www.iuniverse.com
1-800-Authors (1-800-288-4677)

Because of the dynamic nature of the Internet, any web addresses or links contained in this book may have changed since publication and may no longer be valid. The views expressed in this work are solely those of the author and do not necessarily reflect the views of the publisher, and the publisher hereby disclaims any responsibility for them.

Any people depicted in stock imagery provided by Thinkstock are models, and such images are being used for illustrative purposes only.
Certain stock imagery © Thinkstock.

ISBN: 978-1-4620-4559-4 (sc)
ISBN: 978-1-4620-4560-0 (ebk)

Printed in the United States of America

iUniverse rev. date: 08/02/2011

THE WRITER

My whole life I have always saw things in a way different from most people. I don't really know why, I just take it as a gift or blessing from God. I have always taken an interest in poetry, writing, and music; which if you ask me go hand and hand. The poems I write are about feelings, experiences, and things that I have seen in life. I hope in my writing that it will touch different people in different ways according to their experiences in life. The hope that someone can say I understand completely what he is saying and can picture it perfectly. I hope that these writings touch you in a way that inspires or helps you through a situation. I ask that you open your mind and let go of the world as you slip into my world.

KEVIE

I have learned that I can only be happy

Through myself

If I don't allow myself happiness

No one else can give me that

Happiness is about the person

A bitter person will never be happy

Simply and plainly because they don't

Want to be happy.

So I look at myself

And say, am I happy with myself

And I am left with, I think yes

Love yourself

Or you will never be able to love someone else

CONTENTS

SPIRITUALITY

Everyone has some spirituality in them weather they know it or not. Some type of spirituality is an important thing. I meditate a lot on things. It may be a situation that has involved me, or maybe something happening in the world. The following poems are based on spiritual feelings and moods. They may help you to push on when times are hard or they may just make you say I understand what he is saying. We as people are peculiar and complicated, and knowing that we are not the only ones going through things helps us to deal with life better.

THROUGH THESE EYES

Out of these eyes I have seen the light

With these eyes guided through the night

These eyes have seen my years as a child

Through all these years, they have seen a while

Through all the years, the good the bad

Every single one even happy and sad

My eyes have seen it all

The summer, winter, spring, and fall

They have seen birth, the gift of life

They have seen death, the ending of life

All around the world these eyes have seen

For these eyes alone know where they have been

Shed tears of joy and tears of hurt

The value of these eyes

Priceless they are worth

So when they see and close the last time

In peace I will rest these eyes of mine.

FAITH

How strong is my faith

I must be able to trust in god

For things that no man can do

It only requires a mustard seed of faith

And god will do good things for you

God wants to see us succeed

But we can only succeed through him

You can have things but without gods grace

Those things mean nothing

You can have lots of worldly and material things

Without God's peace and grace you won't be able to enjoy them.

There will always be an obstacle in the way

God grants you a peace to know that he is with you and there is everlasting peace.

A world without worries and doubt.

But we must have faith in god.

We all have problems, some more than others.

But one thing is for sure

Those of us who have faith

Put our problems in gods hands and

Don't worry our selves to death

We know the lord will fix it, if it is his will.

If not then there is a reason for it better than we know.

I GIVE THANKS

I thank you lord for my will to live

My prosperity, generosity, and blessings you give

The gift to write, express my feelings,

And touch other people

For they too know these dealings

A mind of reason

Strong at will

Yet reasonable enough to know when to yield

A body that is healthy, and full of drive

Which helps me in life to push and to strive

The understanding of people

As if to read their mind

Understand body language, each and every sign

To have great patience

Understand their wants and their needs

To know the difference between desire and greed

However

I ask that you work with me

To be better and to see

The things I do wrong

Sometimes when I am headstrong

For perfect I am not

The will would be of steel and really take a lot

So forgive me when i sin

And show flaws and weakness that I have got

Just make me better as a man

And mold my mind to understand

LETS BE REAL

Lets be real

Lets lay down the real deal

No more beating around the bush

It's about time for a push

Lets tell the truth

Be real, and let loose

Be real, something on your mind

Something you want to say

To help you unwind

You're holding back

And that's a true fact

I'm not asking much

Honesty is all

Things like that and such

There's a lot on your chest

So don't play the game

Don't poke and test

We're all grown here

Lets be fair

Just let it all out

That's what being real is all about

So lets hear it

The truth and nothing but the truth

Can you do that?

If nothing else you do

Be real

To me, yourself

And anyone else left

STAYING STRONG

Even though there are things I regret

There are those in life I won't forget

A special place in my mind they hold

A part of me burned into my soul

My inspiration that keeps me going

The vision to show me what I'm doing

The will to survive

And to stay alive

To do things right

Weather the storm with all my might

Even though some will be wrong

To learn from mistakes get up and move on

To never ever let it get me down

Or hold my head down to the ground

To always look for the good

And not just the I wish I could

To live up to what I am expected to be

To truly live up to god in me

HOPE

I hope that someday

All things will be well

I hope that someday

Everyone will excel

Dreams will come true

For everyone

Not just me and you

For it's for everyone to enjoy

The peace of mind it can employ

Hope

The wishes of things to come

No thoughts of the past

Or of what has been done

I hold hope for all mankind

As days go by

And we pass the time

END TIMES

In the beginning there was the word

And the word was good

Even though people didn't always do what they should

Time dwelled on and people rebelled

And on the earth was a living hell

Then came the flood and washed things clean

That leads to today

This here scene

The day of the devil

The day of the bad

The day of the mad

Day of the sad

All in misery, everything in dismay

The true portrait of the world today

People strive to excel

To make it to hell

Hail and farewell

The soul that fell

And i keep thinking, keep on watching

The mark of the beast

The unholy feast

The young die young, blind and dumb

Never saw anything that was coming

Clear as day

But fogged to sight, right as light

But dark as night

Temptations beyond, deals that are done

Or has the devil nearly won

OUT OF CONCERN

I write this not out of hate but out of concern, concern of what we have become.

The things I see trouble me.

The way we treat each other. On a day-to-day basis we walk all over each other.

Scratching and fighting to make it to the top. To hold status or power.

What we really do is hurt each other and ourselves in the long run.

I'm troubled because you don't see the games of manipulation.

The tactics that are used to control our minds and decisions.

This is a battle of free will.

You must understand that a freethinking person is the most unpredictable person you can deal with. You can't have any idea of what they are thinking or what they might do.

To be a freethinking person is a good thing. Continue to think for yourself and not just follow the norm. Out of concern is why this bothers me.

I have to live in this world like others who are probably concerned too.

WHERE IS OUR SOCIETY GOING

Since the beginning of time we have always wanted all the answers. How did we come about? Where are we headed? What does life have in store for me, and most of all why? We have spent so much time trying to answer the obvious questions that we strive for nothing in life. Mankind has become so smart that we now want to play god. We want to create the human being ourselves. Forget about a man and a woman we will create it in a test tube. I wonder which direction could that stray us. Are we doing for the better or for worse? We already spend most of our time in a rush. I'm late for this late for that, i don't have enough time for that; there's not enough time in the day. Yes there is its just that society has deemed certain things priority and certain things a waste. Do you know that society spends as much time at work than they ever do in a lifetime with their family? Have you ever really stopped and added it up? And we wonder why the youth are the way they are today. Most of them are raising themselves or a daycare is raising them for us. That is sad someone else spends more time with your child than you do. That means they know your child better than you do. This means your child's bond with that person is just as strong if not stronger than with you. Disbelieve if you want but take a minute and think about it.

Playing outside is basically a thing of the past for children. We now have a substitute parent, the video game. It occupies them and keeps them busy. Most of all the parents don't have to watch them; less responsibility. I wonder what's happening to the youth of today. We have made it where children run the household. Time out took a good old butt whipping out of the picture. I would go ahead and do what I was not supposed to do, if the only punishment I received was standing in the corner. It doesn't hurt. There is no real price to pay, and no lesson to be learned; except that standing in the corner is no big deal. If I had the idea of having my butt spanked there's a bigger incentive to do what I'm told. Prime example; go in any grocery store and watch the moms take a beating from the child. Where is society taking us?

THINK ABOUT IT

This next section is meant to make you think. It is meant to make you see the things that we don't see during our full speed ahead lifestyles. Think about what is being said and understand the things that we take for granted. The things we see but don't see. The things we look over every day and choose not to acknowledge. So slow down take your time and think about it. All the stuff you never paid attention to right in front of your face.

THE SECRETS OF THE EYES

The eyes the doorway to the soul

They always tell the truth when you behold

The eyes a thing of beauty

No one can understand things they can do to thee

Not a word has to be said

The eyes spell it all out in your head

Once connected can not be broken

Nothing need be said not a word spoken

A look can freeze or melt you on sight

One look can disappoint or excite

Something so strange

Not noticed to others

It connects together

Two who are lovers

For the eyes can never lie

Even though the head can deny

A lot can be learned from the eyes

Are they cunning, sleepy, or bright?

Or do they seem to smile and invite

Or do they push you away

And leave you nothing to say

Can they be mistook

I seem to think not

But maybe I am wrong

But i will go on

For wisdom shows in the eyes

Emotion shows in the eyes

Pain shows in the eyes

Even desire shows in the eyes

And all without a word said

Truly a miracle when not misled

So I stop at this and leave it at that

When the eyes speak

The answer is always reached

<u>LIFE</u>

It begins from the time of birth

From the very first breath

An exhilarating burst

From childhood

The experiences you learn

All a part of life as it burns

Through mistakes and learning

We live to be better

It goes on through all conditions

All type weather

Life's many experiences

Strengthens the mind

And shapes individual hearts

Through out a lifetime

Though its roads may sometimes get rough

And it seems the times will always be tough

It makes you the person that you are

Each one a thinking, feeling super star

Life, a funny thing some say

Something that begins and ends every day

Something that can be so happy, so sad

Can be so pleasant yet make you so mad.

Though sometimes frustration sets in

Life pushes on cause frustration can't win.

HUMAN NATURE

The thought crossed my mind

As I've watched people over time

The nature of the beast

The way we don't care the least

The things these eyes have seen

The wrongs committed by human beings

Makes you wonder where we went wrong

And how long will it last or go on

Is society doomed are we nearing our end

In a time of hate among family and friends

The ease and use of disconcern

The greatest of hate does burn

And i never bothered anybody

So why hate me

Were all the same beneath the skin underneath

Wouldn't it be good to all get along?

But we all seem to think that path is wrong

And why

I may never understand

For we are all called human man

INSIDE MY MIND

In my mind

I can be anyone I want

In my mind there is no such things as do's and don'ts

My mind is always working

Things on my mind

I often find myself

Drifting through time

My mind carries me places I have never been

Helps me to sort things out through thick and thin

Sometimes I think to myself

Does the mind control aspects of health?

Is the mind truly the center?

The mind doesn't control what is in us

Is that the job of the heart?

What controls, what in part

For the mind is a terrible thing to waste

But it's done everyday at an accelerated pace

When you broaden the mind

Open your eyes and stop being blind

Use your mind and think for yourself

And in the shadows you'll never be left.

KEEP ON KEEPING

KEEP ON KEEPING

Don't stop moving up

Strive for the best and you will always be good

Learn not to settle for less than you deserve

Good enough is not good enough if you feel you deserve more

KEEP ON KEEPING

When you stop moving a lot of things catch up

Bad luck, old age, doubt, and laziness

If you are on the move those things will always be behind you

An idle mind is a wasted mind

It was made to constantly be thinking and challenged

There is a name for an idle mind…vegative state or paralyzed

KEEP ON KEEPING

Believe in yourself

If you never try to achieve

You won't know if you can

Waiting till later gives you one result

NOTHING

KEEP ON KEEPING

NO PARTICULAR PLACE

On a constant and steady path

In a direction not yet determined

I often find myself wondering

What is the reason?

And what is the season

Will I find purpose and meaning?

Why is this question asked?

For we all have to know

Or have an idea of the big show

Isn't that what life is after all

a series of events

Different times, days, and years

Different moods, decisions, and fears

You may ask where this leads

But where does any of this lead

I think no particular place

THE KEY

Free your mind and your body will follow

The soul is the key

To us not being hollow

For a hollow man can never understand

Nor reach for a higher being in this land

Enlighten yourself

Take care of your health

And so shall follow things and wealth

A state of mind is us being

And so shall it help in seeing

The path

The way

And what to say each day

For a long time

I've searched and looked to find

What was locked down inside my mind

LIFE'S JOURNEY

Through life I have learned

In life I have yearned

For life and that it is

For life and all that it gives

For things that I have enjoyed

And things I have not

In ways I gained a little

In ways I have gained a lot

My life was shaped and molded by life

I am who I am because of lessons in life

It's sad to say that there is so much to learn

Every path in life every way you turn

Life never stops teaching you lessons

Life never stops bringing you blessings

Life is all about what you make

But don't let life be about what you take

Your life is just that

The plain simple fact

So paint the picture of yourself

Make every moment beautiful

From birth to death

And in the end

Life is all there

You decide the who, what, when, and where

TIME

Time is something I may never understand

It neither waits nor stops for no man

But it seems to know when to slow

Or speed up real fast and go

Time fly's when you're having fun

I often wonder can time run

Occupying time is quite the task

For those who have time to pass

Or no particular hour to arrive

But time does tell on all who are alive

Is time just a figment of the imagination?

Something we mention in a conversation

Something we have accepted to be true

Because it gives up purpose and things to do

And the older we get

The faster time gets

What if there was no time

What would we do to amuse the mind?

I guess just wait and sit around

To see when time would come through town

MANKIND

Mankind

Has let me down every time

How we constantly hurt each other

Surprises my mind

The two words don't match

What can you find about man that is kind

We continue to have hope

But it seems that hope is broke

I'm almost tired of hoping

Where there is nothing but hate

And I'm tired of coping

To write our fate

How will it end?

What does the future hold?

How will it end?

When our story is told

THE FLOWER

I looked at a flower the other day

And think I finally realized their beauty.

Something I don't think I've ever really paid attention to

But did see it.

I don't know if it was the place, time, or just me

But the beauty that a flower holds was seen

Not just seen but understood, felt and accepted.

Just the way it was put together the color of the pedals, something made me realize that I had always overlooked its purpose and its qualities.

It seems to put me at peace with the world and myself.

The one peaceful moment looking at the flower.

No thoughts about the world, problems, or situations; just peace. And just think this all came about through a flower.

FREE YOURSELF

Let the soul be free

The spirit be at ease

Body and mind well pleased

Lift yourself above and beyond

Don't worry about things did or done

Peace, peace, and pleasure

Secret to life a golden treasure

Let it be

So easy to see

Free, free, free

Understand nature

For none should hate you

When balance is achieved

All stress is relieved

I say free yourself

It's good for your health

Worration, and aggravation

Are both in relation

So throw them aside

And enjoy for a while

It doesn't come with ease

But it will change you to believe

Open your eyes

Worry no longer

The weak gets weaker

And the strong get stronger

So think of yourself

Your well being and health

Be free

You'll see

Don't just take it from me

TAKE A STEP BACK WITH ME

I invite you to come take a walk back in time with me. Let the world you know now go.

I ask you to set back let your imagination take you to when you were a kid. While you do that think about the youth you see today. I ask you to see a little of yourself in a young person that you see, know, or have criticized. Youth is a beautiful thing and so is growing up. That's why I ask that you help someone young to find that beauty.

YOUTH

I can remember when I was a child

Young and innocent

Without sin

A beginning in life

No idea or care of right

No cares or concerns

No wants or yearns

The best time of life

No black or white

All things done

Concerned around fun

A day went so slow

But little did I know

In time it would increase

And the decrease of peace

Worries and pain

Kevie L. Anderson

Constantly remain

From day to day

To strive to make a way

To try and do what's right

Don't argue or fight

For as I look back

And see the innocence we lack

I yearn for youth

The innocence the truth

That we had when we were young

The days of play, play, and run

I miss it

Youth that is

The one thing you lose the longer you live.

<u>GROWING UP</u>

It's a funny thing to see people immature

Not really caring clean or unpure

Not a single thought on their mind

Not a shred of responsibility not a sign.

They don't have problems

Or it is they just don't care.

Sometimes it amazes me, I stop and stare

 Me, me, is their only concern.

Where's the fun? Is for what they yearn.

And the idea of not having it makes them insecure.

Try taking it away, you'll see for sure.

Then I think back in time, back in my mind.

Was I once in their place, the same unconcerned face?

The good thing about this you see, some look and dismiss

But it helps me realize by seeing through my eyes

What its like to feel pure, to grow up and mature.

YOUR DESTINY

No matter what road we take.

We always seem to end up going in the direction which

Is long before determined for us.

We learn things that help us through these many journeys

And though we may never understand.

Always remember, the good things to come

For a rich man born rich will

Never known anything but richness

And a poor man, poor and receiving richness,

With wisdom wears richness in a whole different manner.

So follow your path and stay steady on the road

No matter how far or heavy the load

For your destiny is set for you

It's there for you no matter what you do

ME BEING ME

I hope that you understand

The nature of human man

The moods, and attitudes

Things we say and things we do

Learn to deal

And not to break my will

For I hope that you can see

That's just me being me

I am the person I am

That will not change no mam

So let me be

Learn to live with me

Let me know the things I do

That hurt and bothers you

And maybe the way things are done will change

Kevie L. Anderson

I am willing to try

Even though they might seem strange

For having an open mind is good

Helps you to not be misunderstood

But on some things let me be

For that's just me being me

When I need time alone

And rather everyone else gone

Let it go

For you really don't know

What's on my mind?

Or if I just need to unwind

Thoughts of things

People, places, and things

Things I need to think about

And maybe later be talked out

But now I'd rather be alone

No people, conversations, or phones

Maybe a moment to be free

Or maybe it's just me being me

So be patient

We will make it through

For all we say, and all we do

Like every leaf has a tree

I will always be me being me

LETS FALL IN LOVE

We have all experienced love in our life. If it wasn't love than we at least thought it was. It could have been infatuation but it was close enough to love that we didn't care. Love can make you feel as though you are on cloud nine. On the other hand love can make you feel like your heart has split into two pieces. Needless to say we have all experienced love. As you read these poems think about how love made you feel. I do hope that you enjoy yourself.

LOVE

The experience

The experience of love

Feelings of the heart

Feelings of love from ending to start

The full feeling of joy

The happiness in the air

Love helps you forget life's despairs

Take away all cares and concerns

For each other is all you yearn

No worries, no need

Take heed

For your feelings shall indeed

Be true and pure

Strong and sure

Kevie L. Anderson

For some won't understand

The matter at hand

For the heart struck one

It's priority one

MATTERS OF THE HEART

Matters of the heart

Such a touchy subject

Can cause such pain

And such joy the same

Can leave you bare

And unaware

Once the candle is lit

With matters of the heart

You never forget

The heart

It sustains life in a beat

But love can make the heart so weak

A heart can be broken

And in time it will mend

But you never forget to the end

Matters of the heart

While together

Or when you are apart

EMOTION

The touch the feel

Anticipation, imagination

What? What?

The feel of joy

The feel of pleasure

How does it measure?

Could it be planned?

Or is it play by ear

What will happen next?

No one knows

Of course not!

Isn't it better that way?

Not a word

Nothing describes it

Only the moment can explain

The situation

The atmosphere

Don't you wish you were here?

<u>BREATHLESS</u>

How can I explain?

The way you make me feel remains

The thought of you on my mind

Gives pleasure to my manly design

The things that you do

The love that you show is true

With you i am whole

You fulfill my spirit and soul

My mind at ease

You are my equal

My half

You make me happy, mad, and sad

The part of my world

My love, wife, and girl

The one I deal with most

The one on my mind when i boast

We have adapted to each other

To become both friends and lovers

Through all the times

And the test

You still leave me breathless

TELL ME

Tell me

I ask you tell me

What pleases you?

Makes you calm

And eases you

Puts you at peace

Helps your worries to cease

Tell me

Help me to understand

So I can see and maybe plan

For in my hopes

Dreams and desires

In an effort to raise emotions higher

Tell me

I beg you tell me

The things you think of

Kevie L. Anderson

Is it hate, passion, or love?

Out of respect for you

Which I will always do

Help me to become better

With the writing of each and every letter

I aspire, I burn, and I yearn

If only you would tell me

So that I can learn

I plead, I beg with all my heart

And pick my brain

Each and every part

But without your help I will never see

So I ask you once again to tell me

THE GAME

I can see you

And maybe you can see me

But we will never acknowledge that

Instead we act as if we don't even know

The other one is there

What is this game we play

And what is the purpose

If as, though to elude

Entice and suffice

To see who will play the hand through

Or will we walk away without a word or two

We all play the game

But not all the same

Maybe a glance

And a slight chance

The language of the body

A test of one another to see

But the question at hand

Is how far will the game be ran

And what will the end result be

Or will the game even be played to see

<u>ECTASY</u>

From the first look

Only a moment it took

The feeling inside

Even though you tried

Your eyes could never hide

Desires and hopes

Started from the first time you spoke

Where will it lead?

Where will it go?

All the way

But no one can say

The first touch

A spine tingling rush

The tingle of the spine

The rush of the mind

Smooth as though made by design

Things we will never understand

How the body can be affected

By the touch of the hand

A kiss

Sends you head over hills

Breaks you down and take all your will

Beyond the point of stop

As your heart rate rises

And doesn't drop

Sensations in places you'd rather not say

In ways and peaks

Not achieved every day

Headed to the place of ultimate pleasure

Place not spoken of

But yet treasured

You shake, you cringe, and you quiver

Fluids flow there like a river

Then calm sets in

You feel peace deep within

A peace of being free

For you have experienced

Ectasy

THINGS ARE GOING WRONG

To exist in the world today is a constant and conflicting challenge. The line between right and wrong has almost in a sense been erased. I don't think we take time to think about what we do and the consequences. There is so much wrong in the world today that we can't tell the difference. I mean to have kindness in your heart is considered a weakness. The matter at hand is that the world needs some care and concern. Think about it, seriously, where will the world be in say ten years at the rate we are going. Ask yourself will killing, robbing, and stealing be something we consider normal. Oh well, enough said; turn the page and journey.

THE FEELING OF SORROW

I am hurting

I feel pain for the world

For the innocent, the naive,

And the unknowing

For those who won't open their eyes to see

For those who can't think for themselves clearly

There is so much going on

A world in dismay

And a world of wrong

All confused, clouded in the mind

Blinded to the facts by design

So many

The victims are plenty

But they have no idea of who they be

Simple in the mind, and in their life

Their mere existence

I ask why

Where does this leave us

Or where does this take us

For a tear I cry

And I cannot deny

All I can do, is ask the lord oh why?

For I see no hope

For the people we are

Because all the answers seem so far

Will we ever see?

Or will we ever be

What god has meant for us to be

LESS FORTUNATE

Open my eyes

And see what I see

The true colors of the world

And what it could be

The death the demise

The hurt in our eyes

When I go in the zone

I feel the pain to the bone

You see you can't understand

Think, glance and stare

They make a snide remark

Walk away and depart

But have you ever really thought

Who that person is or used to be

They could have once been you or me

So don't be so quick to judge

Kevie L. Anderson

Bad things happen to good people

Luck has no sides

Good or bad we all fall equal

You see just because you are where

You are

Doesn't mean you will stay there

For the fall from the top is very far

Even though you were once the star

So the next time you turn your nose up

At someone down

Imagine you are the one on the ground

Oh yes, it can happen

In the blink of an eye

Did and done

Before you can speak and ask why

Don't put yourself above the worst

Just thank god

But see if you can help first

The world is a messed up place

Don't let a picture of that

Include your face

I HAVE SEEN THE SIGNS

What is the world coming to?

What makes us do the things that we do

The hate, we rape

The spirits we break

We crush one another and don't hesitate

This is hourly, minutes, seconds

Not just daily

Where oh, where is the world taking me

I have seen the signs

The signs are here

The days of fear

The end is near

The weather, natural occurrences

Earthquakes, all disturbances

The earth is breaking us down

Opening under our feet the ground

In places we never thought

Places of beauty and peace we sought

Is the earth we destroyed

Showing us our wrongs

But seven times greater and seven times strong

A way of fighting back to survive

Something we have almost killed

Trying to stay alive

The bible speaks of these things, look clearly

Take just a moment to think and hear me

Blinded by the pace of life

We forget about things

Such as wrong and right

I can't help but to wonder why

Why is our world such a total lie

The end is near

I say take heed

A head on collision

Straight ahead full speed

Can't you see?

Or would you rather not see

Where we are headed and about to be

I have seen the signs

The signs are here

The days of fear

The end is near

Fighting in every country

Even small territories

Living and telling their own war stories

Millions die

And usually for a lie

When it's time to stop

And ask yourself why

The carelessness, the disregard for life

The struggles brought about

Through greed and strife

Where will it end?

When will enough be enough?

Or is living in peace simply to ruff

I have seen the signs

The signs are here

The days of fear

The end is near

I can see it clearly

You mean no one else can

The end is coming

Brought about by man

The senseless killings

The young, old, they are bold

The loss of the spirit

The loss of the soul

But it's blamed on so many different things

Except the obvious reason

That remains

Some might say they couldn't help themselves

COME JOURNEY WITH ME

The devil walks the earth

Not just dwelling in hell

And the day is near

Not long, not long

But nobody knows

Who can say who's wrong?

But the signs are there

So, so clear

They are in the bible

To let us know it's near

I have seen the signs

The signs are here

The days of fear

The end is near

To the church before i end

It's a place full of sin

And the price will be great

In the very end

Lead the sheep the books of the bible say

But the path you lead instead

Is dead

The church is not a bank, social club,

Or place of rank

And should not be run by a check that is blank

It's supposed to be sacred

A place of worship

You took this concept

Soiled it and torched it

Sacred doors open for everyone

Made to cleanse everyone

Daughter and son

But instead you shut those you call sinners out

Make them outcast

And fill them full of doubt

How are you supposed to come home?

When the doors are closed

Is there an answer for that?

If so who knows?

The holier than thou

They hold the keys

Most to proud to bow down

To pray on their knees

And the hypocrites that judge and point

The finger alone

Let the one without sin cast the first stone

I ask the lord help me get it right

I grab the paper and pen

And write all night

As in holy worship, meditation

I put all these words into conversation

So it can be heard

Through speaking of words

The rejuvenation brought about through the holy
blood

And maybe we will see how it is supposed to be

Change our way of being to right

So we can clearly see only then

Will god smile down on us?

Stop the fights and the fuss

And things will stop getting worse

Kevie L. Anderson

I have seen the signs

The signs are here

The days of fear

The end is near